MEMBER OF CONGRESS

By Jacqueline Laks Gorman
Reading consultant: Susan Nations, M.Ed.,
author/literacy coach/consultant in literacy development

Please visit our web site at www.garethstevens.com
For a free color catalog describing our list of high-quality books,
call 1-800-542-2595 (USA) or 1-800-387-3178 (Canada). Our fax: 1-877-542-2596

Library of Congress Cataloging-in-Publication Data

Gorman, Jacqueline Laks, 1955–
    Member of Congress / by Jacqueline Laks Gorman ; reading consultant, Susan Nations.
        p. cm. — (Know your government)
    Includes bibliographical references and index.
    ISBN-10: 1-4339-0094-7   ISBN-13: 978-1-4339-0094-5 (lib bdg.)
    ISBN-10: 1-4339-0122-6   ISBN-13: 978-1-4339-0122-5 (soft cover)
        1. United States. Congress—Juvenile literature.   2. Legislators—United States—Juvenile literature.
    3. United States—Politics and government—Juvenile literature. I. Nations, Susan. II. Title.
    JK1025.G67   2008
    328.73—dc22   2008035070

This edition first published in 2009 by
Weekly Reader® Books
An Imprint of Gareth Stevens Publishing
1 Reader's Digest Road
Pleasantville, NY 10570-7000 USA

Executive Managing Editor: Lisa M. Herrington
Editors: Barbara Kiely Miller and Brian Fitzgerald
Creative Director: Lisa Donovan
Senior Designer: Keith Plechaty
Photo Researchers: Charlene Pinckney and Diane Laska-Swanke
Publisher: Keith Garton

Photo credits: cover & title page © Mike Theiler/Reuters/Corbis; p. 5 White House photo by Shealah Craighead;
p. 6 Ron Edmonds/AP; p. 7 Shutterstock; p. 9 Manuel Balce Ceneta/AP; p. 10 White House photo by Tina
Hager; p. 11 Shutterstock; p. 12 Photo by Spc. Grant Okubo; p. 13 Douglas C. Pizac/AP; p. 15 Dennis Cook/
AP; p. 16 © Kean Collection/Getty Images; p. 17 Joe Raedle/Getty Images; p. 18 Courtesy Barack Obama;
p. 19 © Stock Montage, Inc.; p. 20 © New York Times Co./Getty Images; p. 21 Kathy Willens/AP.

Printed in the United States of America

1 2 3 4 5 6 7 8 9 10 09 08

Cover photo: Nancy Pelosi has been a representative from California since 1987. She is the Speaker of the
House of Representatives—the most powerful position in Congress.

TABLE OF CONTENTS

Words that appear in the glossary are printed in
boldface type the first time they appear in the text.

CHAPTER 1

What Is Congress?

Congress is an important part of the **federal**, or national, government. Congress makes the laws for the country. Congress has two parts: the Senate and the House of Representatives. Each state **elects**, or chooses, members of Congress.

Men and women who serve in the Senate are called **senators**. There are 100 senators. Each of the 50 states has two senators. Each senator represents his or her whole state.

Each January, the president makes an important speech before all the members of Congress.

In 2007, Nancy Pelosi was named Speaker of the House of Representatives. She is the first woman to hold that important job.

There are 435 members of the House of Representatives. Each state has at least one **representative**. States that have more people have more representatives.

Most representatives do not serve all the people in their state. They represent people in one part of the state.

All members of Congress work in Washington, D.C. They meet in the U.S. Capitol building.

Members of Congress live in two places. Part of the time, they live in Washington, D.C. They live in their home state the rest of the time.

Members of Congress meet in the U.S. Capitol building in Washington D.C.

CHAPTER 2

What Does Congress Do?

The main job of Congress is to make laws. An idea for a new law is called a **bill**. Any member of Congress can suggest a bill. A bill goes through many steps before it becomes a law. Both parts of Congress study the bill and vote on it.

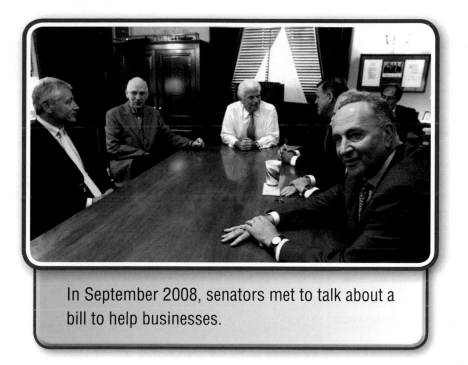

In September 2008, senators met to talk about a bill to help businesses.

If a senator writes a bill, other senators study it. Then the Senate votes on it. If most senators vote for the bill, it goes to the House. The House studies the bill and votes, too. For a bill to pass, most representatives must also vote for it. The bill is still not a law. It needs to go to the president.

In 2004, members of Congress watched President George W. Bush sign a bill into law. The law helped children who have trouble learning.

HIGH STANDARDS FOR EVERY CHILD

If the president signs the bill, it becomes a law. The president may not like the bill. He may **veto**, or refuse to sign, it. Congress can vote on the bill again. Two-thirds of both the House and Senate must approve it. Then the bill finally becomes a law!

Congress also decides how the government will spend its money. Congress works with the president on the **budget**. The budget is a plan for how the government will spend and raise money. The budget includes money for schools, health care, and other important services.

A lot of the money in the federal budget goes to schools.

Congress often holds hearings to talk about the war in Iraq.

Members of Congress also hold hearings to talk about important issues. They study problems in the country and look for ways to solve them.

Congress must also approve **treaties**, or agreements with other countries. Senators approve people the president chooses for some government jobs.

Members of Congress also help the people in their home states or districts. Senators and representatives visit their home states often. They talk to the people they represent. They find out what the people need and make sure the government helps them.

In August 2006, Senator Orrin Hatch spoke to people from his home state of Utah.

CHAPTER 3

How Do People Become Members of Congress?

To become a senator, a person must be at least 30 years old. He or she must have been a **citizen** of the United States for at least nine years. The person must live in the state he or she wants to represent.

Representatives must be at least 25 years old. They must have been citizens for at least seven years. They must live in their home district.

In 2006, the new members of Congress posed on the steps of the Capitol building.

Members of the House of Representatives run for election every two years. Senators run every six years. All members of Congress can run for office as many times as they want. Some people have been in Congress for many years.

People who run for office are called **candidates**. Candidates for Congress share their ideas in many ways. They travel around their state or district. They talk to voters and give speeches. They have **debates** with other candidates.

In 1858, Abraham Lincoln (left) and Stephen Douglas (right) ran for the Senate from Illinois. They had several debates to share their ideas.

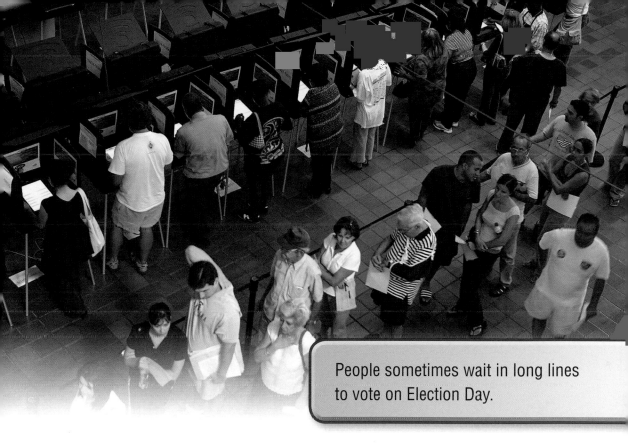

People sometimes wait in long lines to vote on Election Day.

Election Day is in early November. People go to schools and other places in their town to vote. People vote for the candidate they like best. The candidate with the most votes is elected. New members of Congress take over in January.

CHAPTER 4

Famous Members of Congress

Many members of Congress have done great things for the country. Many served in Congress for years and years. Some members of Congress even went on to become president.

President Barack Obama is a former senator from the state of Illinois.

John Quincy Adams was the sixth president of the United States. Before he became president, Adams was a senator.

After Adams was president, he became a representative for 18 years. He is the only president to serve in the House after being president. Adams fought against slavery as a member of Congress.

John Quincy Adams was president from 1825 to 1829.

In 1916, Jeannette Rankin became the first woman ever elected to Congress.

Jeannette Rankin was the first woman to serve in Congress. In 1916, she was elected as a representative from Montana. Since then, many other women have been elected to Congress.

Hillary Rodham Clinton is married to former President Bill Clinton. She was the first lady of the United States from 1993 to 2001. In 2000, she ran for the Senate and won. She is the only former first lady to be elected to office. Like all members of Congress, she worked to make the country stronger.

Senator Hillary Rodham Clinton (with husband Bill Clinton) represented New York state.

Glossary

bill: a written plan for a new law

budget: a plan for how to spend and make money

candidates: people who are running for office

citizen: an official member of a country who has certain rights, such as voting

debates: formal arguments between candidates about where they stand on important issues

elects: chooses leaders by voting

federal: national. The federal government is the government of the whole United States.

representative: a member of the House of Representatives, one of the two parts of Congress

senators: members of the Senate, one of the two parts of Congress

treaties: agreements made between countries

veto: to refuse to approve

To Find Out More

Books

The Capitol Building. Our Nation's Pride (series).
Darlene R. Stille (Looking Glass Library, 2008)

Hillary Rodham Clinton: Dreams Taking Flight.
Kathleen Krull (Simon & Schuster, 2008)

What's Congress? First Guide to Government (series).
Nancy Harris (Heinemann, 2007)

Web Sites

Congress for Kids
www.congressforkids.net
This site explains how both parts of Congress work and what they do.

Kids in the House
clerkkids.house.gov
Take a trip around the Capitol building and learn about Congress
and how laws are made.

Publisher's note to educators and parents: Our editors have carefully reviewed these
web sites to ensure that they are suitable for children. Many web sites change frequently,
however, and we cannot guarantee that a site's future contents will continue to meet
our high standards of quality and educational value. Be advised that children should be
closely supervised whenever they access the Internet.

Index

About the Author

Jacqueline Laks Gorman is a writer and an editor. She grew up in New York City. She has worked on many kinds of books and has written several children's series. She lives with her husband, David, and children, Colin and Caitlin, in DeKalb, Illinois. She registered to vote when she turned 18 and votes in every election.